Tudor Theatre

Moira Butterfield

W

FRANKLIN WATTS

LONDON·SYDNEY

Designer Jason Billin
Editor Sarah Ridley
Art Director Jonathan Hair
Editor-in-Chief John C. Miles
Picture research Diana Morris

First published in 2006
by Franklin Watts
338 Euston Road
London NW1 3BH

Franklin Watts Australia
Hachette Children's Books
Level 17/207 Kent Street
Sydney NSW 2000

ISBN-10: 0 7496 6452 5
ISBN-13: 978 0 7496 6452 7

A CIP catalogue record for this book
is available from the British Library.

Printed in China

Dewey classification number: 792'.0942

Note to parents and teachers:
Every effort has been made by the Publishers to ensure
that the websites in this book are suitable for children, that
they are of the highest educational value, and that they
contain no inappropriate or offensive material. However,
because of the nature of the Internet, it is impossible to
guarantee that the contents of these sites will not be
altered. We strongly advise that Internet access is
supervised by a responsible adult.

Contents

The first theatres

The first British theatre was built in the 16th century during the reign of England's queen Elizabeth I (1558-1603).

Many of the plays written and performed at that time have become world famous and are still performed today. Of all the Tudor playwrights, William Shakespeare is the most well known.

Before theatres

Before theatres were built bands of travelling players (actors) travelled the country. They would put up a temporary stage and perform in a town square, the cobbled yard of an inn or the hall of a large house, and the audience would pay to see them. Early travelling players would probably have performed their own versions of traditional stories that everybody knew, such as Robin Hood or a story from the Bible.

Queen Elizabeth I loved watching plays and encouraged the growth of the theatre.

Key fact

Elizabeth I belonged to the Tudor family, who reigned for 118 years. Her successor, James I, became king on Elizabeth's death. He belonged to the Stuart family.

Theatre is born

The Burbage family were theatrical businessmen and they were the first people to build a permanent theatre. It was simply called "the Theatre", and it was built in Shoreditch, London, in 1576. It was round in shape, with most of the seating in balconies, overlooking the stage. Some people also stood in the yard in front of the stage for the performance.

Theatre is a hit

People flocked to see plays at the new theatre. Building on this success, new groups of actors, called companies, formed in London and more theatres were built for them to perform in. Acting companies had to get permission to perform from royal officials, so they were only allowed to exist if they pleased the Queen and her nobles.

 Did you know?

Travelling players used to go to Stratford-upon-Avon, where William Shakespeare grew up. He would have seen their performances.

 Go and visit

Travelling players performed outdoors, even in fields if they had to. You can go and see a Shakespeare play outdoors every summer at Hyde Park in London, and at other venues around the country.

Travelling players often performed on a temporary stage in the yard of an inn.

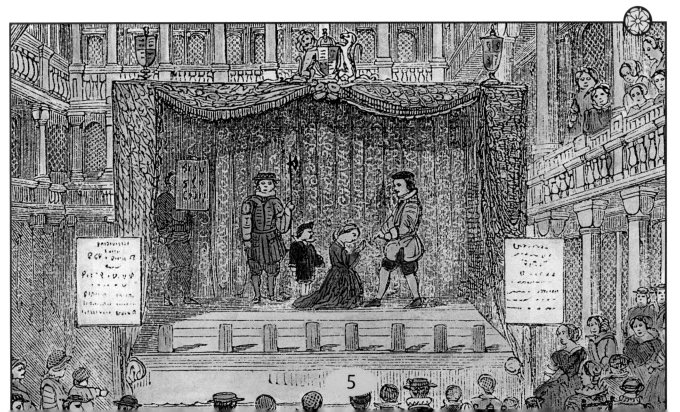

Off to see a play

London was the biggest city in England at the time, and it became the centre of theatre life.

The main entertainment area was Bankside, a road along the south bank of the River Thames in an area called Southwark. Several theatres were built there, including Shakespeare's theatre, the Globe.

Theatres mean trouble
The area of London called the City was controlled by officials who thought plays were immoral and likely to bring rowdy troublesome crowds. They also disliked the nobles who backed the acting companies, so they banned theatres from within the City walls. Bankside was outside the walls, so the theatres there were safe from interference.

Party across the river
The new theatres gave themselves names, such as the Rose, the Swan and the Globe. Playgoers could walk across London Bridge, or pay a penny to catch a ferry across the Thames to see a performance. Once in Southwark they could also go to taverns for a drink or join noisy, excited crowds at a bear-baiting pit.

This drawing shows the original Globe Theatre, on Bankside in London.

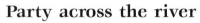

Come to the play

When a play was going to be performed, a flag flew on top of the theatre for everybody to see. Plays were performed in the afternoon, so the audience could get home before dark. There were no plays on Sundays or for two months in summer, when London was a hot and stinking place and there was a danger that deadly plague might spread amongst the crowd.

This sketch was made in 1590 and shows the stage and some of the seating in the Swan Theatre. The Globe probably looked similar inside.

 Go and visit

You can still walk along the south bank of the River Thames, and see the City on the other side. Visit the the replica of Shakespeare's Globe Theatre, a reconstruction of a 16th-century sailing ship – the 'Golden Hind' – and much more.

 Key fact

Elizabethan theatres in London regularly had to close to try to limit the spread of the disease called plague. Players toured other towns, putting on performances to earn money while the London theatres were closed.

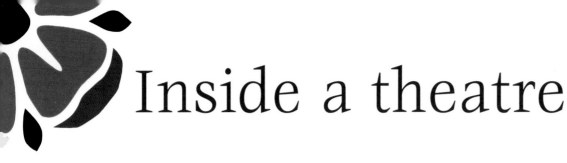

Inside a theatre

The most well-known Elizabethan theatre is the Globe, where many of William Shakespeare's plays were first performed.

The Globe has now been carefully reconstructed, based on drawings and diaries that describe original theatres of the time. It is a working theatre where you can see performances of Shakespeare's plays, along with newer works.

This model of a Tudor theatre shows the stage **1**, the gallery for wealthy nobles or musicians **2** and the seating in the covered balconies **3**.

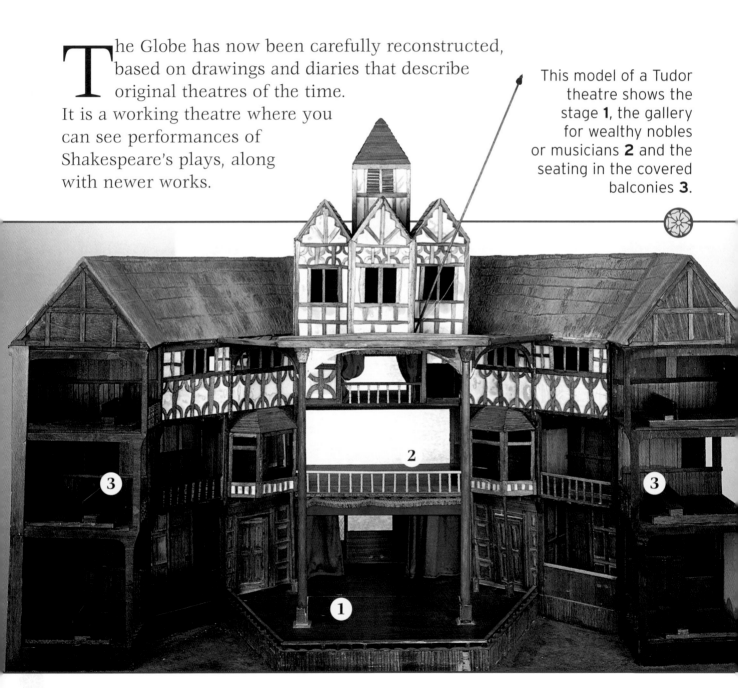

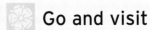

Go and visit

The Globe Theatre in London. It has a museum all about Elizabethan theatre life, and you can visit the stage, which has been rebuilt to look like an original theatre of the time.

In the round

The first theatres were round in shape, and partly open to the sky. The stage jutted out into the central open area, with a small roof over it to shelter the actors. Playgoers could sit in balconies around the edges, or pay less to be "groundlings", standing in the open air in front of the stage. Grand lords and ladies could sit in a balcony at the back of the stage (see page 17), away from the crowd.

Key fact

There are no surviving plans of the old Globe Theatre, but a picture and description of another theatre, called the Swan, do survive. Historians think it was similar to the Globe.

New effects

The roof above the actors was painted with stars and clouds to look like the heavens. It was fitted with ropes so that actors or props could be flown down from the roof, which must have been an exciting new development for Tudor audiences. In the stage floor there was probably a trapdoor for actors to appear and disappear. Fireworks and smoke effects might have been used onstage, too.

Backstage

Backstage there was a "tiring room", where actors changed and got their props. They came onstage through doors (there was no stage curtain). Outside, doormen collected the entrance money in boxes, which is where we get the term "box office". There was no heating, lighting or toilets but playgoers could probably buy snacks.

Did you know?

The groundlings were sometimes nicknamed "stinkards", because the actors could smell them from the stage, especially when it rained and they got wet.

By Royal Command

At Christmas or on special occasions, theatre companies would be commanded to visit the monarch's palace, or the house of a grand noble, to put on a play.

This was a great honour for the actors. Playwrights, such as Shakespeare, wrote plays especially for these special events.

Indoors at last

The play took place in a big room, lit by candles, and the audience of nobles sat in front of the actors, who came in and out of the room's doors. The actors probably enjoyed these occasions. Not only were they warm and dry, they were well paid, and their audience were educated theatre-lovers who appreciated a good performance.

Impressing the nobles

It was vital for a theatre company to impress its powerful audience, because the actors' jobs depended on it. If a theatre company upset the monarch or a noble, they could be banned from working or even thrown in jail.

Nobles gather for a performance by a visiting theatre company.

Did you know?

Acting companies were paid a fee of £10 for a royal performance, much more than they earnt on a normal day at the theatre.

The Chamberlain's Men

Lord Hunsdon was the patron (supporter) of the acting company Shakespeare belonged to. They were called the Chamberlain's Men because Lord Hunsdon was the Lord Chamberlain, an important position in Elizabeth I's Court.

Tudor-style fame

Successful actors and playwrights were celebrities in Elizabethan times and nobles did not mind mixing with them. After a Court performance, the main theatre actors would probably be invited to dine with the nobles themselves. The lesser actors would be invited to eat in the royal kitchens.

Key fact

Elizabeth I had several London palaces, reached by boat along the Thames. Acting companies had to make sure they were based near enough to the river to easily reach the Court if they were commanded to appear.

Go and visit

Hampton Court, a rare example of a surviving Tudor palace, is on the Thames. You can still take a river boat from the centre of London to Hampton Court. Other Elizabethan palaces included St James, Whitehall, Greenwich, Richmond and Westminster.

A depiction of how Elizabeth I and her courtiers might have watched a play being performed in a grand house.

11

The theatre company

There were several different companies of actors working in London in Elizabethan times.

The most famous one of all is the Chamberlain's Men, because their playwright was William Shakespeare. Others included the Admiral's Men, run by Philip Henslowe.

Richard Burbage was a star actor and part-owner of the Chamberlain's Men.

In the company

The co-owners of the company were called "sharers". William Shakespeare was a sharer in the Chamberlain's Men, along with the main actors and manager. There were also boy actors and stagehands. The company would probably have had about twelve adult actors and four boys. Women and girls were not allowed onstage in Tudor times.

Key fact

The main actors, the managers and sharers all shared in the profits of the performances, and probably had a say in the way plays were written and performed.

The main man

The company manager had to make sure the company made more money than it spent. He paid for plays to be written, chose the right actors for the parts and employed people to help put on performances. The manager of Shakespeare's company was Richard Burbage, who was an actor as well as a businessman. He even painted the sets.

Stars of the show

The star actors could probably turn their hand to any part, but some specialised in comedy and had parts written especially for them. In Shakespeare's company the most famous actor was Will Kempe, who was a comic star famous for performing funny dances called jigs.

 Go and visit

A theatre workshop for children, where you can try your hand at being an actor. Most theatres run these, so look out for one near you. Libraries are good places to get this kind of information.

 Did you know?

Occasionally there were fatal accidents on stage, particularly during sword-fights when actors risked being accidentally stabbed to death.

Boys on stage

It was against the law for women or girls to perform onstage in Tudor times.

This was because it was regarded as very wrong for a female to display herself in such a public way. Boys took on the female roles, training to talk and act like women.

Acting apprentices
A promising young actor would be apprenticed to an acting master, one of the main actors in a company. He would live with the actor's family, and would learn to move, sing and dance like a woman. As noblemen had long hair and dressed in fine embroidered clothes and jewellery at this time, it wasn't seen as all that unusual for a male to dress in female clothes.

Childrens' companies
In London there were some acting and singing companies made up entirely of children. For instance, The Children of St Paul's performed in a house near St Paul's Cathedral, and we know they entertained Elizabeth I. The Queen also had her own group of choristers (boy singers) who sang and performed for her.

All boys wore dresses until the age of five in Tudor times.

Key fact

Some boys went to school in Elizabethan times, but girls did not. Many children never went to school at all, but worked from an early age.

Growing up

When a boy actor grew up and his voice broke, his career as a child actor was over. If he was good enough, he might be offered parts as an adult man, but there was no guarantee because his adult voice might be too weak for the stage. Scholars think that, because of their poor diet, Elizabethan boys reached puberty a couple of years later than boys do now. Their voices would probably have broken around the age of 16 or 17.

Did you know?

Boy actors wore heavy make-up and a "bum roll", a padded cushion under their costume to give them a female bottom shape.

 A wealthy Elizabethan woman in typical dress. Boy actors tried to make themselves look as lady-like as possible.

Go and visit

The Museum of Costume in Bath, or the Victoria and Albert Museum in London, to see how the Tudors dressed. Original examples of Elizabethan clothes are on display.

The theatre crowd

Watching a play at an Elizabethan theatre must have been a lively experience. The standing audience shifted around and even joined in, if they felt like it!

All kinds of people went to the theatre, from all walks of life. The balcony seats (also called "galleries") were more expensive than standing in the "pit" in front of the stage, so well-off Tudor people such as merchants and lawyers would probably sit there.

Sixpenny seats

For sixpence, men could actually sit on the side of the stage itself, perhaps to show off their fine clothes. They were very close to the actors and must have been a real nuisance at times! Groundlings paid a penny to stand in the pit (see page 9).

For groundlings, theatre-going was noisy, smelly and often wet.

The "Lord's Room"

The "Lord's Room" was a balcony above the stage for noblemen. They could hear the play from there, but could hardly see it at all. Perhaps they were more interested in being seen at the theatre than in watching the play. When lords and ladies weren't in the Lord's Room, the theatre musicians probably took their place. They accompanied the play performances.

Go and see

A play at the modern Globe. These are held in summer and allow us to get a feeling of the experience of watching Elizabethan theatre, come rain or sun.

Actors perform in a Shakespeare play at the modern Globe Theatre.

Scandal!

The theatre was seen as a scandalous place, where ladies met lovers and where gambling and drinking went on. Many people of the time thought actors were rascals who behaved badly and that theatres were wicked places. As well as plays, theatres such as the Globe put on cock-fights, where baying audiences placed bets on vicious battles to the death between cockerels. For the theatres, it was another way to make much-needed money.

Key fact

A theatre such as the Globe could fit in over 1,000 people at a time, so it must have been very noisy and exciting.

Props and costumes

Each acting company kept a store of props, the objects needed in plays. They were expensive for the actors to buy, so they had to be looked after carefully.

They included such objects as swords, crowns and thrones. The company also owned a few costumes, stored between plays.

Costumes help the audience to understand the actor's part.

The tiring house

The props were kept backstage in the tiring house. The tiring house was also the actors' dressing room. Here the "tire-man" (wardrobe master) was responsible for the props and for the valuable costumes too. On the day of a play he made sure that everything was ready for all the actors. Elizabethan stages didn't have big background scenery. Instead there were small moveable pieces, such as a tree or a bush.

Costumes

The acting company owned and loaned out costumes to the minor actors, but the leading star actors bought their own clothes to wear on stage. Everybody wore normal Elizabethan clothes, never imaginative made-up costumes or costumes from a different era such as actors do nowadays. Sometimes a theatre company bought second-hand clothes, discarded by aristocrats.

Did you know?

Tudor theatres used real cannons to provide special effects. In 1613, a cannon set fire to the thatched roof of the Globe Theatre and it burnt to the ground.

When Tudor plays are performed at the modern Globe Theatre, the costumes are often in the style of Shakespeare's time.

Props of the Admiral's Men

An inventory (list) of props has survived from the Admiral's Men, an acting company of the time. The list includes all kinds of surprising objects, such as a rock, a cage, a tree of golden apples, Neptune's fork, a rainbow, a bull's head and a dragon! There were several crowns and weapons, and even a "black dog". Perhaps it was a painted one, but we don't know for sure.

Key fact

Playwrights would build props into the plays they wrote. Shakespeare's play *Hamlet* uses a famous prop, a skull held up by the actors.

Go and visit

The backstage area of a theatre, to see props and dressing rooms.
Most theatres run tours, including the home of the Royal Shakespeare Company in Shakespeare's home town, Stratford-upon-Avon.

The plays

The acting companies paid playwrights to write new plays for them.

They had to get permission to perform a play and pay for a government licence. If a play was thought to spread dangerous ideas, it would be banned.

Taking a copy

Shakespeare wrote with a quill, a bird's feather dipped in a pot of ink. Once a play was written down, someone at the theatre copied it out once. This precious copy was used to prompt the actors if they forgot their lines during a performance. Play copies were very valuable to a theatre company. Sometimes they were illegally copied and sold, rather like pirate CDs and films today.

Actors and their lines

The actors were given their own part written out separately and stuck on a long piece of parchment. They never had the whole play to read, only their own lines. Each morning the lines for that afternoon's play were handed out for the actors to memorise, or to refresh their memory.

Joseph Fiennes uses a quill pen in a scene from the film *Shakespeare in Love*.

Key fact

The English spoken and written in Shakespeare's time did not sound the same as modern English, and there were lots of words we no longer use. The plays are sometimes hard for modern readers to understand, so modern editions have lots of footnotes that explain what words mean.

Plays worth millions

During Shakespeare's lifetime his plays were printed in pamphlets called quartos. They are the nearest thing we now have to the original manuscripts, which are now lost, but the quartos vary and scholars argue over which is the most accurate copy. The *First Folio*, the first known printed collection of Shakespeare's plays, was published in 1623. Early Shakespeare quartos and folios sell for millions of pounds when they come up for sale.

The title page of the *First Folio* edition of Shakespeare's plays from the British Library.

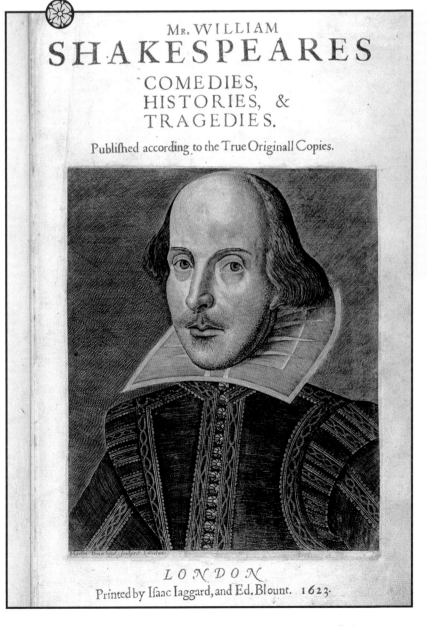

Mr. WILLIAM
SHAKESPEARES
COMEDIES,
HISTORIES, &
TRAGEDIES.

Published according to the True Originall Copies.

LONDON
Printed by Isaac Iaggard, and Ed. Blount. 1623.

Go and visit

The British Library website at www.bl.uk, where you can see photos of some of the priceless Shakespeare folios and quartos kept there.

Did you know?

Some of the most famous lines in Shakespeare vary between quarto copies. Nobody is sure which are the versions copied from Shakespeare's writing, and which are versions made up of lines later remembered by the actors who took part.

William Shakespeare

William Shakespeare is regarded as England's greatest-ever playwright. He wrote history plays, comedies and tragedies, and also wrote short poems called sonnets.

Is this the face of William Shakespeare? The portrait of the playwright in the National Portrait Gallery, London.

He wrote during the reigns of Elizabeth I, and then her successor, James I, who reigned from 1603 to 1625.

Young Shakespeare

Shakespeare was born in Stratford-upon-Avon in Warwickshire in 1564. His father was a glove-maker who became an important local figure in the town. His mother was the daughter of a farmer. Shakespeare probably went to grammar school, where he would have learned to read and write Latin. He married and had children before he went to London to be an actor and a playwright, leaving his family behind.

Key fact

Shakespeare was a big celebrity in his day. His plays were particularly liked by Elizabeth I and James I. After his death, his reputation kept on growing, until he became the world's most famous playwright.

Acting and writing

No-one knows what happened to Shakespeare between 1585 and 1592, when he first moved to London. He was probably a minor actor with different theatre companies. But by 1594 he had joined the Chamberlain's Men and gained a patron (supporter), the powerful courtier, the Earl of Southampton. For the next twenty years he was with the Chamberlain's Men — as their regular playwright — and also owned a share of the Globe. Later, in 1614, he went back to Stratford-upon-Avon and died there two years later.

What did he look like?

We don't know for sure what Shakespeare looked like. Several famous pictures of him were in fact done many years after his death, so could well be wrong. Perhaps the most likely image is on the monument erected on his tomb by his son-in-law. It was put there while Shakespeare's wife was still alive, so it may well be accurate.

The statue of Shakespeare in Westminster Abbey, London.

Did you know?

Some scholars insist that William Shakespeare could not have written the plays which carry his name. They think he was too ill-educated. Several suggestions have been made for alternative writers, mostly nobles of the time.

Go and visit

The tomb of William Shakespeare in Stratford-upon-Avon. In the same town you can visit some of the houses connected with his family. The houses are furnished to show you how the family lived.

Shakespeare's rivals

Shakespeare was not the only Elizabethan playwright. There were several others, including Christopher Marlowe and Ben Jonson.

Christopher Marlowe. Some people think his death was faked and that he lived in Italy for many years after 1593.

They all knew each other and probably met regularly in London venues, one of which was the Mermaid Tavern, near St Paul's Cathedral in the City of London.

Marlowe, murdered star

Marlowe was a theatrical celebrity of the time. He was an actor and playwright, and his plays are still performed today. In 1593 he was stabbed to death at a house in Deptford, near London. Some people think he may have been murdered because he was a government spy. His plays themselves are violent, full of bloodshed, brutality and passion.

Key fact

Ben Jonson trained as a bricklayer before he became an actor. Christopher Marlowe was the son of a Canterbury shoemaker. Just like Shakespeare, they gained success through their talent, but they all had the help of noble patrons, too.

Ben Jonson, in trouble again

Ben Jonson was known for his satires – lively rude plays that poked fun at people. He was an actor, too, and once accidentally killed another actor in a stage duel. He escaped execution, but later found himself in prison again for being rude about the Scots and offending James I (a Scot). In his writings he mentions that his fellow writer, Shakespeare, was proud of the fact that he never made a blot on his writing. Jonson rudely joked that he wished Shakespeare had blotted out more of his awful work! But he also praised Shakespeare, and was probably his friend.

An engraving of a portrait of Ben Jonson.

 Go and visit

The National Portrait Gallery in London, to see pictures of people in Tudor times. Visit the website – www.npg.org.uk – to see thirty portraits of Shakespeare!

Playwright teams

At the beginning of his career, and towards the end of his life, Shakespeare wrote plays jointly with other playwrights. This was probably not unusual for the times, when playwrights often wrote together to get plays done quickly. His final three plays were written with a new young dramatist called John Fletcher. One of these plays, called *Cardenio*, has been lost.

 Marlowe and Jonson

Marlowe's plays include *Tamburlaine the Great* (1587), *The Tragical History of Doctor Faustus* (1589), *The Jew of Malta* (1589) and *Edward II* (1592).

Jonson's plays include *Everyman in his Humour* (1598), *The Alchemist* (1610), *Volpone* (1614) and *Bartholomew Fair* (1614).

Danger!

It was very dangerous to displease a monarch in Shakespeare's time. Acting companies had to be very careful not to perform plays that might offend.

Shakespeare's main personal patron was the Earl of Southampton, a friend of the powerful Earl of Essex. In 1600 the Earl of Essex fell out of favour and was banned from the Court of Elizabeth I. He did not go quietly, and instead sought revenge on her advisors. It was a dangerous time for all those connected with him, including Shakespeare and the Chamberlain's Men.

A risky performance

The Chamberlain's Men took a great risk at the time of Essex's plotting. They performed a controversial play, Shakespeare's *Richard the Second*, for his supporters. It told the story of a monarch who was so badly advised he lost his throne. Soon after the performance, Essex and his men marched through the streets of London, demanding rebellion against the Queen's advisors.

The Earl of Essex had been an extremely close friend of Elizabeth I. However, his desire for power led him into conflict with Elizabeth.

Key fact

All actors and playwrights of the time had to be very careful not to get too involved in the intrigues of the nobles, or they could find themselves in the Tower, banned from performing. Elizabeth I had many spies, ready to report on any disloyal subjects.

The end of Essex

Essex's march failed to get support. He was arrested, imprisoned in the Tower of London, and later executed. Shakespeare and his acting company may only have survived because the Queen forgave them. Perhaps she realised that they had no choice but to obey their patrons. Perhaps it was because she liked their plays so much.

 ## Did you know?

The Chamberlain's Men were commanded to perform at Court on the evening before the execution of the Earl of Essex.

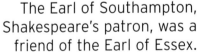

The Earl of Southampton, Shakespeare's patron, was a friend of the Earl of Essex.

 ## Go and visit

The Tower of London, where those accused of disloyalty to the monarch were imprisoned and executed. The Earl of Essex was executed there on 25 February 1601. Shakespeare was lucky to avoid a spell in jail there.

Banned!

Elizabeth I died in 1603. The theatres were closed as a sign of respect during the official mourning period.

When they reopened they were hit by the plague and had to close again. It was the beginning of a tough time for British actors.

The audience gets drunk

Elizabeth's successor, James I, liked the theatre and at the beginning of his reign Shakespeare's popularity was at its height. Gradually, however, the nobles at Court grew more wild and out-of-control. Plays were performed for drunken courtiers, and sometimes even the actors themselves got drunk.

Masques became popular in the early 1600s. This picture shows a masque taking place in the great hall of a large house.

The end of the acting

During James's reign, and under his successor Charles I, masques became more popular than plays at Court. A masque was an evening of music, poems and dancing, in which women of the Court could take part.

The Puritans

The theatres were closed once again during the English Civil War in the 1640s. They were then destroyed by the Puritans, who banned acting and punished actors by whipping them and locking them in the stocks. The Globe was closed down in 1642 and then pulled down completely two years later. Today, the replica of the Globe (below) stands close to the position of the original theatre.

 Key fact

English Puritans of the time thought that acting was wicked, and were always trying to get it banned. They succeeded when they won the English Civil War, and no-one acted again until Charles II came to the throne in 1660. He allowed women on the theatre stage for the first time that we know of.

 Go and visit

The Theatre Museum in Covent Garden, London, or see their collection charting theatre history by going to www.peopleplayuk.org.uk.

GLOSSARY

Apprentice
Someone learning a trade from a more experienced person, such as a boy actor learning from an adult actor.

Admiral's Men
A famous theatre company in Shakespeare's time.

backstage
The area hidden behind a theatre stage, where props and costumes are kept ready, and where actors wait to go onstage.

Bankside
A road running alongside the south bank of the River Thames, where Elizabethan theatres stood.

bear-baiting
A Tudor sport pitting a chained bear against dogs in a fight to the death.

bum roll
A padded cushion that boy-actors wore to give them a more female shape.

City of London
An area of London on the northern bank of the River Thames, inside the original city walls.

Chamberlain's Men
Shakespeare's acting company, who performed at the Globe Theatre.

company
A group of actors who regularly worked together in a theatre.

Elizabethan
During the reign of Queen Elizabeth I, from 1558 to 1603.

folio
A printed collection of Shakespeare's plays.

galleries
Balconies around the inside of a theatre, laid out with benches for the audience to sit on.

Globe, the
The theatre that William Shakespeare co-owned.

groundlings
Members of the audience who stood in front of the stage.

masque
An evening of poetry, music and dancing

patron
A wealthy important person who supported a theatre company, or an individual artist, giving them help at Court if they needed it.

plague
A deadly disease that killed many in Elizabethan times.

player
The Elizabethan word for an actor.

props
Objects used by the actors during a play.

Puritans
People who believed that acting was sinful.

quarto
A printed pamphlet version of a Shakespeare play.

quill
A pen made from a bird's feather.

Southwark
An area of London on the south bank of the River Thames.

sharers
Co-owners of a theatre. Shakespeare was a sharer at the Globe, which meant he had put some of his own money into getting the theatre started.

tiring room
A backstage room where props and costumes were kept by a tire-man and property men.

touring
When an acting company travel around, putting on plays in different towns.

tragedy
A play with an unhappy ending.

Tudor
The name of the family who ruled England for 118 years, including Henry VII, Henry VIII, Edward VI, Mary I and Elizabeth I.

TIMELINE

1485 Henry Tudor defeats Richard III at the Battle of Bosworth Field, bringing an end to the Wars of the Roses. He is crowned King and the Tudor period begins.

1558 Elizabeth I is crowned Queen, the fifth Tudor monarch.

1564 William Shakespeare is born in Stratford-upon-Avon; Christopher Marlowe is born in Canterbury.

1572 Ben Jonson is born in London.

1576 The first theatre is built in England.

1582 Shakespeare marries Anne Hathaway.

1583 Shakespeare's daughter, Susanna, is born.

1585 Shakespeare's twins, Hamnet and Judith, are born.

1593 Christopher Marlowe is killed in Deptford.

1595 Shakespeare is in London and performs in front of the Queen.

1596 Shakespeare's son, Hamnet, dies aged 11.

1599 The Globe Theatre is opened.

1601 The Earl of Essex leads a rebellion and is executed.

1603 Queen Elizabeth dies and James I becomes king. He is from the Stuart family, not the Tudor family, so the Tudor era comes to an end. Theatres are closed until 1604 because of the plague.

1608 The Chamberlain's Men, now renamed the King's Men, open an indoor theatre at Blackfriars, but keep the Globe open.

1613 The Globe burns down, but it is rebuilt.

1614 Shakespeare returns to Stratford-upon-Avon.

1616 Shakespeare dies.

1637 Ben Jonson dies.

1647 The Puritans ban acting.

1660 Charles II comes to the throne, and revives the theatre. The first known woman appears in a stage play in England. Her name was Margaret Hughes.

WEBSITES

www.shakespeares-globe.org
The website home of the reconstructed Globe Theatre.

www.rsc.org.uk
The website of the Royal Shakespeare Company, who perform in London and Stratford-upon-Avon. Find out about their work.

www.shakespeare.org.uk
Find out all about Shakespeare's life and his birthplace.

www.kingedwardvi.warwickshire.sch.uk
The website of the school where Shakespeare was a pupil.

www.nationaltrust.org.uk
Find out about Tudor places to visit near you.

www.britinfo.net/theatre/about.htm
Find a weblink to your local theatre, to see what's on and how you can join in.

INDEX